It is dawn and the sun is rising.
Where is WomWom?

WomWom is sleeping. She is in her burrow.

It is morning. Some animals are hungry. Some animals sleep all night.

Many animals rest and hide. Birds will rest when it is midday.

WomWom is asleep. Some days are hot.

WomWom will stay in her burrow if it is a hot day.

The Sun moves across the sky. It rises in the East and sets in the West.

Sunset is coming and birds are feeding.

Sunset sees many animals come out to feed.

Some animals hide.
Some animals do not sleep at night.

Some animals look for food when it is night. WomWom eats at night.

Sunrise is coming so it is time to sleep. Have a good rest WomWom.